TWO BOWLS OF MILK

BOOKS BY STEPHANIE BOLSTER

White Stone: The Alice Poems (1998)
Two Bowls of Milk (1999)

TWO BOWLS OF MILK

Stephanie Bolster

M&S

Canadian Cataloguing in Publication Data

Bolster, Stephanie
    Two bowls of milk

Poems.
ISBN 0-7710-1557-7

I. Title

PS8553.O479T96 1999   C811'.54   C99-930013-X
PR9199.3.B64T96 1999

We acknowledge the financial support of the Government of Canada through
the Book Publishing Industry Development Program for our publishing
activities. We further acknowledge the support of the Canada Council
for the Arts and the Ontario Arts Council for our publishing program.

Typeset in Galliard by M&S, Toronto
Printed and bound in Canada

McClelland & Stewart Inc.
The Canadian Publishers
481 University Avenue
Toronto, Ontario
M5G 2E9

  2 3 4 5   03 02 01 00 99

For Patrick Leroux

CONTENTS

COME TO THE EDGE

Come to the edge of the barn the property really begins there,
you see things defining themselves, the hoofprints left by sheep,
the slope of the roof, each feather against each feather on each goose.
You see the stake with the flap of orange plastic that marks

the beginning of real. I'm showing you this because
I'm sick of the way you clutch the darkness with your hands,
seek invisible fenceposts for guidance, accost spectres.
I'm coming with you because I fear you'll trip

over the string that marks the beginning, you'll lie across the border
and with that view – fields of intricate grain and chiselled mountains,
cold winds already lifting the hairs of your arm – you'll forget your feet,
numb in straw and indefinite dung, and be unable to rise, to walk farther.

My fingers weave so close between yours because I've been there
before, I know the relief of everything, how it eases the mind to learn
shapes it hasn't made, how it eases the feet to know the ground
will persist. See those two bowls of milk, just there,

on the other side of the property line, they're for the cats
that sometimes cross over and are seized by a thirst, they're
to wash your hands in. Lick each finger afterwards. That will be
your first taste, and my finger tracing your lips will be the second.

But few have gotten at the multiplicity of them, how each berry
composes itself of many dark notes, spherical,
swollen, fragile as a world. A blackberry is the colour of a painful
bruise on the upper arm, some internal organ
as yet unnamed. It is shaped to fit
the tip of the tongue, to be a thimble, a dunce cap
for a small mouse. Sometimes it is home to a secret green worm
seeking safety and the power of surprise. Sometimes it plunks
into a river and takes on water.
Fishes nibble it.

The bushes themselves ramble like a grandmother's sentences,
giving birth to their own sharpness. Picking the berries
must be a tactful conversation
of gloved hands. Otherwise your fingers will bleed
the berries' purple tongue; otherwise thorns
will pierce your own blank skin. Best to be on the safe side,
the outside of the bush. Inside might lurk
nests of yellowjackets; rabid bats; other,
larger hands on the same search.

The flavour is its own reward, like kissing the whole world
at once, rivers, willows, bugs and all, until your swollen
lips tingle. It's like waking up
to discover the language you used to speak
is gibberish, and you have never really
loved. But this does not matter because you have
married this fruit, mellifluous, brutal, and ripe.

4

SEAWOLF INSIDE ITS OWN DORSAL FIN

Seawolf Inside Its Own Dorsal Fin, Robert Davidson, 1983. Screenprint.

I sleep in the red of my rising
arc, curled tight and finned

within fin, rocked by black
water I rock. I learn this one part

of myself, each degree
of its curve, how the water

foams against warm skin.
My fin learns me, the thing

it is part of but does not
belong to. We make each other,

my fin and myself, myself
and the taut water.

When my fin breaks the sea's
skin, through shut eyes I glimpse

wave within wave, stone
within stone, I surge

through all the layers,
my own incessant crest.

This dome opened
the year of my birth.
My whole life stands
on this wooden bridge, arched
over water.

Below, plump and golden
fish ripen.

Foliage, hushed as silk, encroaches.

ASSORTED FLORA

Nasturtiums

Always plural,
rampant.

Edible because
something must be finished off,

your unflinching
ruffled orange and gold,
your tart leaves.

Even aphids will not
do the trick.
Even inclement weather.

Even in October
you assert yourselves,

outdoing the leaves,
the smug pumpkins.

Iris

Your spine is a secret grief.

Rooted in inconstant mud,
you manage to stand, proud

though purple marks the perfect
white of your throat.

But cut, left
alone in a vase, you will lean

away from light, shrink
into your crippled shadow.

Beach Sweet Pea

Tenacious as cat's claws
you cling to the salt
grit, mark your place

in roots and the innermost
pink of anemone's
tentacles. Beside that dropped

starfish with its guts to the sky,
that branch bleached
and sea-worn,

you are the one
who holds brine between your toes,
tide in your teeth.

Oriental Poppy

The truth is in the red of you,
the black centre wide
as a pupil in a blind-drawn room.

Bloodshot, you stare
into the sky and will not squint
until the sun does.

RED STILETTO

"Poetry: three mismatched shoes at the entrance of a dark alley."
    – Charles Simic, "Our Angelic Ancestor"

Something here –
Nike runner with its arc
of dreamed flight, feathered
bedroom slipper, red
stiletto with the pointed toe,
arrows into darkness.

The bodies have hopped between
dumpsters, between these bookshelves.
Hissing cats, torn pages, milk
cartons licked blank.

They have unwritten
their other legs. They believe in silence
and the striving after balance.

Somewhere in there
they stand like resting flamingoes,
tuck around them
the memory of the other leg
like a cruel friendship

lost in childhood. Phantom phrases still
caught in their knotted tongues.

ASSONANCE

Hurt bird in dirt – she writes
for sound, and a sparrow

that hit the window of her childhood
too hard. Because of how the ear

takes words in and holds them
to itself, how they strike

those bones: *hammer, anvil*
and *stirrup*. Words that conjure

machinery, weight,
horses, that morning her leg

caught and the mare dragged her
for miles. From the first,

each word she'd learned
a hoof just missing her

temple. It is all pain,
the reddish shell the side

of the head cups, and hears
itself, hears itself.

Stunted remnants of plants, months-old dogshit, a single red mitten that belonged to a girl who'd been punished for the loss, one hand made to go bare the rest of that winter. When her mother, tending tulip shoots, found the mitten, she pinned it to the girl's chest, broke the skin so she would not forget. The next winter they found the girl's heart, grey and hard as stone, in the centre of a thrown snowball. It nearly blinded the boy. In the kitchen they set the heart beside the turkey wishbone, meatless and saved for later. Microwaved on low, stroked with new white towels, it thawed into the pumping of nothing through itself. In the hospital they returned it wrapped in sheets and anaesthesia, stitched deep, a gift she could not return. The next year she went walking in her red rubber boots until only a trail of hollow exclamation marks was left.

By the lake I find a mole unearthed, mouth raw as supermarket steak. Its body is a cylinder furred with the passive half of Velcro. Its feet curled pink as a bird's.

A friend says he has killed two mice in as many days. He wakes to the snap and finds one caught behind the eyes, dancing its last dance. Afterwards it's hardly a heft in his palm, less than a skipping stone.

I find the fish plucked eyeless and scaleless where the tide has left. It might have been perch or flounder, might have been angelfish. Wind stirs no inch of it. Sand sifts around it. This is the longest its fins have been anywhere.

When I visit my friend, a car hits a crow, and the street's a sudden gathering of crows. For half an hour outside his window black eyes watch the curb and that black unflapping thing. Then they're gone. I leave behind my half-drained teacup.

This evening each thing dies before me. A bundle of muddy newsprint is a chewed raccoon's tail and those distant blown shreds of tire by the roadside, what's left of a bear.

How could I not turn away from the precious bald head of that man waiting in the bus shelter?

Tamarack, shamrock,
black water with a stone in its throat. Black willow:
Very shade-intolerant. Branches brittle and breakage

frequent. Limbs under water. Black ash: *Neither as strong nor
hard as white ash wood.* Black hawk falling. Squirrel call. Teeth against
teeth against hunger. Variations of predation. What's swallowed

still warm in the throat. I don't want the names of vegetation
in my mouth, only his tongue, his different speech. Variations
of flight and flightlessness. Crows are rooks, but rooks

are sharper and still blacker. Nettles can make healing
teas. Bluebells by the river ringing someone's
gone too far.

Hills are islands, waiting. Mountains
will wait longer. This valley

was once a lake, until we made it land. See how the rain
against the windshield turns to fishes.

Each puddle a premonition. The woman's face
is clearer there. When I peer in,

the trees shift. The sky is bluer
than the sky and when I look deeper there is the sun.

Any rain is enough to make all the colours
come out. The fuchsias sting my eyes

and the bees shine. The lawn teems with drops
that might be diamonds, might be frogs.

—

The first time I ran inside and shut my house. The second
I let it all wash over me. The third time I went looking

where the clouds were and weeks later
waded back with minnows in my boots.

Between storms: a segment of train track. A red
block with the letter O. A mouse the colour

of bread mould. An ace of spades. Three steps going down
and who knows how many underwater.

I keep a canoe on the back porch just in case.
Each morning I listen for the lap against the bedposts.

Each morning I imagine my legs floating down the steps,
my hair seeping back from my face.

—

Watering the garden, I call the earth thirsty
and then cringe at what I've said. The way things are

is simpler and more difficult to understand. My throat
and the columbines open for the same water differently.

Closed rose petals, a sky not scrawled with cloud,
the small of the back, these are lesser. Beauty is the red

rectangle of a barn surrounded by flood.
The white chicken on the rooftop testing its wings.

—

When the first drop falls, she is there
to meet it. The underside of her arm is a fish's belly,

her mouth a rain gauge. She is the watermark
and the water rising.

Her rusted car. Where the road was, a river the colour of asphalt.
A rag doll is growing heavier beside her boat. Beneath,

a catfish looms. Farther down, street signs
and streets, yellow lines down the centre.

—

Two-thirds of the earth is composed of water,
not counting floods. I'm more water than this world is.

Maybe that explains the shift of my organs
during sleep, the glass beside my bed.

The curve of the boat's hold
is the shape my hand makes

when it wants something. How quickly
my palm fills when I stop asking.

TWO BOWLS OF MILK

Are two bowls of milk. They are round
and white and have nothing to do

with the moon. They have no implications
of blindness, or sight. They wait

on the doorstep like bowls
or like things that closely resemble

bowls in their stillness. The bowls do not
foreshadow cats. There are two

because two hands set them out
and each wanted to hold something.

Milk because not water. The curve of
milk against the curve of bowl.

PERSPECTIVE IS AN ATTEMPT

FLOOD, DEER LAKE, B.C.

I'm out in it. The water's ruddy
with the seepage of needles
fallen from towering fir. Ice
floats thinly in it, and slush,

and patches of snow farther
back in the trees I came from.
It's shallower there. Here reaches
midway to my knees, here

where the path was last week.
My parents have hung back
in soggy boots, but mine
can take it. I might go farther

still, not around the lake,
as we planned, but into.
The water's clear white, flat,
under slivers of ice a duck broke,

landing. It laps at the brown rubber
of my boots, cedar trunks.
When was I not out there?
If I leave here, where will I be?

When the first wasp would not stop flying near me I sat still
and let it stay. All thin legs and yellow, it did not find my skin
but the silvered mouth of the Pepsi can. It crawled inside

and then another joined it there. I let those two
fill themselves while I finished my greasy knish and thought
how I would soon not be here and how painful

not wanting anyone. One wasp staggered out
and flew, and then the other, and in Manhattan
they were two cabs on their way in one direction. Inside,

what I had loved most: the folds of the woman's scarf
in Vermeer's portrait, their depth of shadow,
how the fabric came so close to itself without touching.

NATAL

Woman in Blue Reading a Letter, Johannes Vermeer, c. 1662-64. Oil on canvas.

I've been told she is not pregnant, but regard:
I mean not only look at her but hold her in esteem,
because her heft of belly cannot be attributed to style
or the way her bluish smock rucks up
under her breasts. She would not otherwise hold
the letter at that height, above the swell,
to protect her child from grief. She would not let

the windowlight fall over all that new weight, fall
on the cold within. I would not say a man has written,
the lover from a wide distance,
husband, unsuspecting, coming from the colonies,
father or her brother who will not help.
It might be her mother: *come to me.*
Or the girl she giggled with when thinner,
now with one at each breast.

It's long since she was singular and stood
with her forehead warm against the glass, her waist
to the ledge with no flinching tenderness.
Soon she will be forced down and open
and then what rooms will let her and the other in?
Take care, she's not herself these days
or ever was. To let go of an emptiness
so large, to look upon and love it, how could she not
require the light? The panes divide her and divide.

Because Vermeer looked into a room and saw a map was lit,
I now find it possible to sit here: my shutters flung to sun on brick
on the apartment across the street, where the man rocks
before the blue-draped lamp. Light falls on my pictures
of salal and fern still growing elsewhere (home is not this frozen
sparrow on the porch, an icicle across my sight)

and the girl with the turban, who is always turning.
There's not long left. She already misses
who she's witnessing lose her. Because in keeping her still
for several days Vermeer saw the changes and broke
in trying to retain them, the crooked hairs of her brow
and the brush of scarf against shoulder.

He lit mostly the far side of her face, it would be gone
first. Soon he'd have only the nape, and her back
receding. Soon the map would dim and crumple.
I have folded it myself, often, bringing this place near
to where I'm from, but there is still the shadow between
and a difference of time. Here the streetlamps stutter on.
There it's still light on my mother's turned face.

WHITE ROCK

My mother said they saw the droves of fish uncoil,
she and my father far out over the water at White Rock
where I used to follow them into the wind.

The fish passed beneath the pier, a quick stream
until they gathered close, whirled around each other
to elongate again and go. The whole school moved

as one creature but the human crowd dispersed,
most watching instead the taut lines, gulls
raiding the bait. Had I been there, we would have been three

bent over the rail, trying for that depth and that
fluidity, the three of us seen from behind recognizably
of the same source and unspeaking, worshipping.

CHEMISTRY

Instantaneous Photographs of Splashes, Arthur M. Worthington, 1908. Gelatin
silver collage.

Inept in everything except perception – and even there
subjective – I'm only partially my chemist father: I never
threatened to explode my childhood with experiments

but watched my mother release a blot of half-and-half
into the glass cup that held her coffee and a hurricane
ensued before her spoon dipped in to smooth things out.

When photographed with utmost care – the care my father,
demonstrating for his students, gave to filling his pipette
and counting tears of danger as they mixed with mildness –

a drop of water falling forty centimetres
into a bowl of shallow milk will make a rising
circle, widening until a phallus strains upward

from the centre, milk and water bound.
With its tip congealed into a sphere, the column falls back,
the globe drops in and the milk is a little more

watery. This quick gift's gone unglimpsed as I wash dishes –
my hands dank in gloves – and muse on some dumb
wall of brick. Across the continent my father watches

another sitcom while my mother waits for my next call.
Each time she reaches the ringing first: my words travel four
thousand kilometres to the saucer of her ear.

By the time I speak to him I've achieved that even
surface, coveted aftermath of his childhood combinations:
after the bang and froth is that silence we both live beneath,

small water fallen into so much milk.

LUGGIE

In my palm a photograph of me, holding
in my palm the huge gold salmonberry –

it's summer, the bush behind us
only beginning to turn to luxury houses,

and I have a small room with my name
on the door, a brother and parents

who love me. I picked this fruit because
I wanted to own its size and yellow sheen,

because we called it *luggie* for its luminous
bursting. What did we think,

naming it? It makes no sense.
My mother coaxes me to eat it.

My father thinks it worthy
of a photograph; my brother believes

it's magic. It has nothing to do with me.
That it's yellow instead of ordinary red,

that I found it, means nothing. It is just
what it is. Its taste would leave me

as I was, as I am, as I was, as I am.

VIRGINIA WOOLF'S MOTHER IN THE BLURRED GARDEN

A Beautiful Vision, June 1872, Julia Margaret Cameron. Photograph.

Ten years before your birth, you already live
in her face, in the sharpness of her nose,
the omniscience of her eyes. Your longing for solitude

permeates her, emanates from her like moonlight
to blur the camera's focus.

Behind her, blossoms quiver, shrink
into their nightly state, leave her alone.

You are not even thought of, and yet she is thinking of you
here with the tendrils of vine at the nape of her neck.
Her eyes sting with salt wind, though the sea
is miles distant, the air draped and still.
She sees, as if through layers of gauze

or water, desires worn to ragged
skin beneath waves. She widens her eyes
against crying, and the shutter blinks

her into permanence. Light spills from her
like ocean water. The mouth

of time gapes wide
and chokes.

You saw the battered fear on the woman's face
as she witnessed herself in the mirror, parting
her long hair like a raven preening feathers,
expecting someone behind. And then you didn't see her,

only her reflection, which you'd inherited
when your sleeping eyelids twitched and you slipped
into her skin. Now your hands lift to bruises,
your heart quickens but your feet won't go.

You don't know what came before,
only the certainty of fist raised or scissors
held to your hair. That glint the corner of your eye finds,
which turns to plain sunlight when confronted.

You've forgotten what dreams are. No words
can fill the open mouth the mirror shows you, these lips
now yours: numb as gutted fish, wide with the knowledge
that this moment cannot be awoken from.

FARGO IN FLOOD

I've never been to any of my favourite places
but I saw the film, that north American town
ensconced in snow. A pregnant woman stood
on a blood-flecked plain beside a car wreck,

pronounced a man dead. Now, like all those
grey roads in my sleep, Fargo's under water.
Minnows pass through open windows
of that upturned car, lodge in the dead

man's pockets. The current sways him as if
he were alive, in love. Somewhere, the actress
from the film stands by a river with her son,
that swelling within her on the movie screen now

actual. On another channel, Manitoba grows heavy,
towel darkening with spill. I dream
of ghostly birch immersed, roots nudging up.
Those women in the wreckage, seeking

photographs of children, will find
life's become a soggy matter in their hands,
no one's to blame. I wake to red
on threadbare sheets, another thin blue sky.

NOONS

Too many hours beside him on the bed are never enough.
Outside is the sun's old light, inside its dim reaches.
The bleached hills out the window

are not Crete. Heat is an indoor pleasure,
snow heaped in the courtyard over the *balançoire*.
She dreams alien neighbours and wakes to their footsteps.

Easier even than the warmth of his sleep
is her own tunnelling in. Her skin wall-white
as though she's seen something terrible.

FLOOD, NEAR JOLIETTE, QUÉBEC

The thousand snow geese lift over the flooded plain
as we drive by, my love, my mother and I remarking on the glint
given by underside of flight, white feather reflecting
water on field reflecting wing. Others shimmer by the hundreds
where water shouldn't be. That the earth would give this
to thank them for returning is miraculous.
The farmer has his own word to describe it.

That my mother should be here with us for a time, having flown
across this continent of shield and accidental lakes, that I
should live here now, is what the geese pay tribute to.
Yes, I apologize for the struggle of crops. Yes, I recognize

that beauty can violate another wholeness. But that turn of flock
over flood, I can't say it is not alone enough
to compensate the waist-deep trees. And so I bear witness
and so my burdens lift. We are here.

DEUX PERSONNAGES DANS LA NUIT

poems from paintings by Jean Paul Lemieux
(b. 1904 Québec, d. 1990 Québec)

INTÉRIEUR (1930)

Till now you've picked a self each day:
sharp-tongued cynic, innocent, fool in love

with how his face distorts in polished
bedposts. In a lake my features

shift: there shy girl, there mindless, there
adolescent with a crease between her brows.

Each shadow my profile casts on page
or yours on canvas makes another face

to live within. Until tonight: this mirror's
frozen you in charcoal grey, you've traced

your shades to find despair becomes you.
You should not have turned your brush

upon yourself so soon. My shadow's grown
still darker, will not lighten. How finally

we're caught, those roses in the wallpaper
half-open into wings of flightless moths.

LE TRAIN DE MIDI (1956)

On first entering the white
field, I think I'm dead, and this

no heaven. Aftertaste of sacrifice:
I've left the coast, crossed Rockies,

plains and shield to sleep beside
my love and learn his tongue.

Born here in winter, you nod
welcome, let me stand beside you

to watch the train pass. We aren't
going anywhere. I had not known:

that Norway of your idol
Munch no country of the mind,

so dark just after noon he
couldn't paint in more redeeming

shades. *C'est triste, la neige* –
your words freeze and drop.

When you lie dead in December
in a white bed, you will be no

angel rising, only a slow
sublimation: snow becoming

vapour without ever being
water. Now I'm winter's daughter.

LES BEAUX JOURS (1937)

Here a glimpse of soaring blue: her scarf,
flicker of summer maples against river.

This Madeleine you've married, will she
make you remember who you were

before cold weather? With grace her sun-
burned neck bends to the view you paint

her into. This morning she laid aside
her brush to make your lunch

and has not picked it up again.
(Before your death she'll speak

of sacrifice as though it were a pool,
blood-warm, and I will read her archived

words, furious in winter.) Whose
choice was this? Though you

believed her praising eye alone
kept your canvases alive, you killed

the part of her that could have lit you.
Love bends me in more resistant shapes;

my neck cracks like ice. I would not give you
a shred of blue, my own too few and far.

LE FAR-WEST (1955)

A few acres of snow. In a Montréal
December I come upon your few feet

of west, a tawny field grazed on
by some animals. They might be

antelope and this some view of
Africa – or cows and Idaho? What

cowboy hat do you imagine
my umbrella is? You have not gone

far enough, your English Bay a mouth
drawn shut, its trees cowering

under an enormous Québec
sky I cannot write, my words

small glimpses between
this branch of fir and that. How west

must have threatened to open
you. My pages nearly white

these days, I'm shutting up.
That "I" I write no longer me

but you, alone in the midst of what
I call nothing and you home.

L'ORPHELINE (1956)

Whatever makes you and I believe
ourselves *tout seul* has got her too,

her painted face the unrepentant
grey of moon. I know lead

lines her eyes, each chamber
of her heart. Her eyelashes rubbed out:

this world the same no matter what.
I cried till I had no water left. All was

ice. Those rectangles, a distant
steeple: what home crumbled into

when I left. Parents might be waiting
at a kitchen table for her safe return,

very much alive, as mine are, as yours
were when you turned them into

monuments apart. You hardly left
the city of your birth, never arrived.

Though I made it holy in my mind,
that place I left was never mine.

LE CHAMP DE TRÈFLES (1971)

Where did summer come from,
the field awash in clover? A woman

I should know is placed just so, as all
your women are, elegant and self-

contained, extending in her hand
wildflowers a blue I thought extinct.

Her colours layered upon your old
palette over grey and black make

your eyes tear up. Her lips rise into
a smile you had not foreseen. Can you

reach to meet her hand? All of this
is yours. You scratch your name, small

near the edge of her white dress,
then trade this canvas for another,

blank. If I turn from you and take her
offered luck, will this sky break?

LA FLORIDE (1965)

This couple used by sun then left
behind could be your parents,

old: his face driftwood whittled
too long, hers a blob of cocoa butter.

That place of snow and mapled
beans, kitchen with its crucifix,

might not be real from here. The boy
a sheaf of wheat behind them,

midday hot on the back of his head,
turned away. Why is he here?

He's looking at that scatter of small
figures far down the sand.

He could go there. But you didn't,
you became that downcast

man who casts no shadow under
unrelenting sun. I could have turned

into her, hat wide-brimmed to keep
my face from melting. Instead I'm

so distant I might be a grain of sand
or the water my feet enter.

1910 REMEMBERED (1962)

You remember yourself: boy, aged
six, striped into a sailor suit alone

between two figures: *la mère, le père.*
You have not changed, painting

that cloud a stone above your head,
approach of hope as a woman

under her white parasol. She might
save you, if the sky doesn't fall before

her steps draw near. Listen: I've feared
earthquakes, falling asteroids, being

alone. Let your fingers span that
distance to the crenellated edges

of your mother's parasol. We're
loved. Your wife sitting in the garden

as you paint, my love calling me
in his magic accent. Our mothers

never leave us. Toward that promise
on your flat horizon I've walked

under overcast sky, then out. Sun
bathes me, forgives my doubt.

DEUX PERSONNAGES DANS LA NUIT (*V.* 1989)

This is only part of it: red smear
of her lips at the left, his at the right.

Which is longer, winter
or the distance between them?

How little they like each other, how
alike they look. Soon you will

leave us with this, no spare room
in the wide frame for your wife's

body close through twenty thousand
nights. I wait with her downstairs

in the kitchen where she taught
children how to paint. We clink

our glasses of red wine, liquid jewels
lighting the white cloth. In that field,

you're still waiting for the train.
Why did we believe we needed

tickets? Why didn't you walk? Here,
a fire melts snow from my socks.

LES BEAUX JOURS, REPRISE

Tu me manques to my English
mind means "you are missing

from me." But I don't miss you
and am whole as I cross this white

plain that is the river. Water
holds me up. This was blue

just months ago, rippled, and will
soon return to ripples to return

to sea. You were dead when I
first saw your painted faces

taking numbness as their due.
They still loom up, open

their mouths, too weak to break
through ice. I do not bend

to crack open breath-holes
I could fall into. Home is my feet

laying a path I'll follow back.
Sun streams through a buoyant

sky to dazzle snow. My shadow
flits, so quick it can't be fixed.

INSIDE A TENT OF SKIN

poems in the National Gallery of Canada

FLAP ANATOMY

The Ingenious Machine of Nature: Four Centuries of Art and Anatomy, National
Gallery of Canada, Autumn 1996.

Nothing is unsplit.
In the cabinet of flap anatomies,
babies burst through women's paper
flesh full-term, germinated
through some random crash of cells.

Framed upon the wall, fathers frolic
in various degrees of nude
and skeleton and écorché, muscle
stripped like bacon from their thighs.

My jutting pelvic bones
injure my lover, scare children
from my lap – I might be that dissected
girl in pen and ink, perused

by a dark-suited man who smells
of hot secretions. He examines each
of her named parts, then my narrow waist.
Does he imagine the soft gap
that lies inside? I must be oblivious to it, I am

a brain aloft within a skull. I have seen
skunks torn to a stink of crimson,
white and black; Frère André's heart
in glass; but not the inside

of my body. Opened like that woman
a hyena's jaw tore into while she watched
or the yellow-fever victim
who vomited his stomach out,

could I claim those ruddy clots
and pulses as mine, as me?
Could I look upon my insides, out?

STILL LIFE WITH BRAID

Female Dissected Body, Seen From the Back, Gérard de Lairesse, 1685. Engraving
with etching.

I loved her when we washed our hands
in matching sinks at school. She feared the cubicles
where a raincoat with a man in it might stand
on a toilet's rim awaiting us, pocket knife

tight in his fist. Once her desk waited
all day for her. She was not dead, the teacher
reassured, just camping with her family. I doused
my tears in icy water, wished for her braids.

She did not come. My letter slot released
a drawing of an iris, pencilled throat open, bulb
engorged beneath. Veins so intricately etched
they stung the purple in my wrists. No hand but hers

had done it. Then I forgot. Time passed
until I visited a gallery and ticking stopped
before her adult portrait: wrists resplendent, raw
in bracelets of taut rope. A posture

she had practised during recess to prepare.
Peeled to reveal her braided spine, skin draped
her waist, was pinned aside like coy sleeves fitted
to her upper arms. The alphabet named her

crucial points but not that curl she'd tucked
behind her ear at eight. Her face averted, ashamed
at believing its body worth this spectacle of death.
Why did I not tell her she was more than this? I am

no more myself: bones pitched inside a tent of skin;
fear; one bound hand and the other binding.

OUT/CAST

September 1975, Colette Whiten, 1975. Plaster, burlap, wood, rope, fibreglass, metal, and paint.

Flesh was here: eyes shut under
sticky white, whorl of ear within
which plaster hardened, muting

all sound. All that remains
is the space a woman once took.
What if these sarcophagal hinges

swung shut, enclosing my whole
body? A ship inside a bottle, but
who outside could pull the string

to lift its sails? Once, on a Gulf
island, my friend pressed wet sheets
of plaster against my face until

my face was there without me.
Later she painted rose and yellow
over that hard white and on her

cabin wall I didn't recognize
myself. The air around her naked
body as she showered in the forest

glistened. Two profiles engaged
with each other make a curving vase
between them. One face that shuts

itself into a box has made a box.
It was so dark that I was blind
to shapes my face engraved inside.

DOG-WOMAN

Dog-Woman, Peggy Ekagina, c. 1974. Greyish-green stone.

Who's to say I'm not
that dog, that small
woman low to ground

and wrought of greenish
stone, packed inside
the flaccid palm of who

I think I am. Snow
and blue ice, song
of a woman cutting

excess from a rock
she found. She kept it
warm a long time in her

fist, the idea of dog-
woman hardening
to bone, barking hot.

It took her a week.
Ice cracked, her kids
cried for meat. Now

dog-woman lives
in a glass case in
a basement where a girl's

paid to wear a suit
and watch that no one
steals her. I come

on Fridays. That girl and I
have nearly melted
the glass with our breath

waiting for animal speech.
In silence, dog-woman's
replete, unleashed.

WAITING ROOM

The Hotel Eden, Joseph Cornell, 1945. Assemblage with music box.

Mornings, a green parrot pronounces children's names in French. This room is white and past the glass a clutch of palm trees waves hello, goodbye. Then there's the sea. I watch it froth. I push that yellow ball across the floor beneath my foot. It puts a good hurt somewhere in my throat. I've read the body's made of bits that link in unexpected ways and this is one: when I say the parrot's name he tugs a string to start the music box. Stars twinkle twinkle as song pricks a metal fingertip. There is no blood. My mother sang that, *twinkle*, very far away. She's even farther now and still I find her voice inside my mouth as I address the box I painted shut. It's not too late to fill it with an infant, little protuberance from my gut. But I have my bird and chair and music, water always moving out. I have the song my mother passed along and cannot give it, ever, up.

SIX NUDES OF NEIL

Neil Weston, 1925, Edward Weston. Photographs.

You frame many parts of him.
Anonymous buttocks, torso

the delicate curvature
of treble clef, he's become

another thing entirely.
Fresh from his mother, he was

all light and stirring; unlike
your vegetables he would not

lie still until the right shadows fell.
Now he lets you prop him

in a doorway. For the last
picture you open the shutter

to let in his face you've placed
in profile. What part of you

made him look like that?
His cheek is desert. It will outlast

all the stones you've photographed.
It's hot, the door is blocked, your

dark clothes hurt you, you have
never loved anyone enough.

GARDEN COURT

In childhood I dreamt I would be in such a still place.
These plants were never pulled from actual
earth, they were always here under pebbled light.
Their leaves are green and paler green, and flowers
bloom an antiseptic pink in rows. Painted,
this would be more than real. Itself, it's less,
a simulation copied from no thing. And I?
What air is here is thin, held under a bell jar.
In the dream, goldfish the colour of blossoms
were under a bridge under a sky, it was a good place.

TO DOLLY

Three Sheep, Alex Colville, 1954. Casein tempera with graphite on masonite.

If that look originates in eyes
identical to yours but not
your eyes, who is watcher

and who watched? All three
might be you, each responding
to the name a child gives

the plastic baby she bestows
her heart and all her hurt upon.
Once my friend – my sister

but for blood – strode toward me
in a café I was not in, in a city
I had left. *You didn't answer*

when I called your name –
she blurted by phone and I,
lost and fraught with guilt,

apologized. If I'd been her,
would the café-me have answered
to myself, then turned away

as Vermeer's girl – anonymous
but for grief – turns from
and to me? Do you, Dolly, take

comfort in that mother,
sister, child whose smell
is you and yours – or want

to vomit out yourself? Soon
you'll fill this field and never be
alone, and that's my fear.

THE BEHELD

The Lovers, Fred Ross, 1950. Tempera with oil glaze on masonite.

Not mine, this woman's nostrils
widening to furry tunnels;
her mouth a cabinet of enamel,
pebbles burrowed in her gums.

Not me, this lip-gape, this neck
he forces back with one of his hands.
Hers clutch each other, in prayer,
in thanks. I know what she wants:

for his heat to melt her freckles,
smooth her brow, restore the nose
she had before she spent an hour
looking in the mirror. For him to see her

perfected like that. For how long
did I adore that photograph of me
and the man I love – lips open
unto each other, shut eyes resplendent –

before he pointed out my nipple
flaring in a corner? I slid the picture
in a drawer, arranged my dress
in folds across my chest. I avoided lenses.

SUM OF OUR PARTS

Ancient Roman Bowl with Early Christian incised Grape Vines transformed into Oil
Lamp with French Empire Mounts. Agate with silver-gilt and gilt bronze mounts.

An object is its story, so: a bowl
was once broken and became this

relic embellished with a maiden –
to hide cracked sardonyx

and burn between her stiff wings
a wick over oil. Encased and labelled,

she pores over an empty bowl
held whole inside a patterned shell of gold.

I am alone. I admire from above,
her arched body not unlike mine

but bare to naked gazes. Then bend
and find the gold that holds her there

(and keeps this elegance together)
is an ancient gorgon mask: mutter

underneath her song, rumble of guts.
Snakes I didn't know I harboured

start to wake; my features, granite,
crack. I have seen. I have been seen.

STOP MOTION

Dropping and Lifting a Handkerchief and *Woman Pouring Bucket of Water
over Another Woman*, Eadweard Muybridge, from *Animal Locomotion*,
1885-86. Collotypes.

A naked woman walking, snap
by snap, drops her handkerchief,
picks it up, moves on, always a step
ahead of me. Farther down the wall,

she pours a bucket of cold water
over another naked woman . . .
naked too the scream when the torrent
hits, although – because – both knew
what was expected.

A man watched through a lens
(her walking, a horse lunging
forward) and clicked to still each change

as it was changing. I follow the fetlock,
swell of the striding woman's calf,
watched by hidden cameras

of the gallery. A guard clicks his metal
counter as I leave the exhibit,
leave behind the air I moved through,
still pretending flow

is true: each wave
that shivers pebbles on the shore is no event,
just continuity, the water slipping back
beneath the froth and smoothing down the stones

for another inrush. I pretended love
was inevitable, as though there were no moment
when a certain neuron clicked and I said *this* –
yes, this – and plunged ahead,

let the handkerchief get muddy
under others' shoes. I picked up the bucket,
angled it above myself and let the icy water
flood me: wondering if anyone was watching –

wanting this image for future
witness: this is me, deciding, permitting
my body to be overtaken.

BLOOD

Atara, Rita Letendre, 1963. Oil on canvas.

A dark metal stinking
through my panties,
stockings, skirt.

Strangers sniff my ability
to bear a child, my deliberate
lack, neglected cave
expelling iron ooze

and shutting up.
What could begin
in that rank enclosure
walled in ruddy moss?

Lascaux's blotched
animals and spears
prove that life is possible.
But I did not come
from that place.

I arrived complete in a white
peroxide box, my name
in pink plastic sealing my wrist.

My horse-shaped birthmark
soon faded. I'm human
once a month.

THREE GODDESSES

I. Fear of Desire

Venus, Lucas Cranach the Elder, c. 1518. Oil on linden.

Love, the Romans said they made you –
and how small you have become.

Barefoot on stones, you have no need
of fig leaves, for you've learned

to keep the body in itself and not to let
the breasts go loose. What child

could your hips span other than yourself?
In fear you've put on heavy necklaces

as though you were not enough. Your
painter must have thought you wanton,

his neck aflush with shame at posing a girl
unclothed for Art. Your shame at having

flesh is greater. Would you rather lack
a body and so be safe from probing

fingertips and gazes, be safe from what
that body wants? I have wanted

to turn away from the sudden ivory
of your skin, too rare a thing,

endangered, endangering its self
and mine by such exposure.

II. Fear of Enormity

Hope I, Gustav Klimt, 1903. Oil on canvas.

Impossible the taut globe of your belly.
What does it not contain? You trust
that each nail, once born, will be
immaculate, as you have become, having

shunned man's touch for months and carried
in your body another body's weight.
Your feet are lost behind some monster
wave of shadow those masks behind you cast:

Death, Decrepitude. Against their knowing
sockets' gaze, you hold your elbows bent
as wings to make a phoenix of your hair.
He hated that your ordinary reddish

freckles turned into a universe of far,
insistent stars, that you were shapely
and misshapen, vertical and utter, and loomed
inside his doorway – his model grown

to distances he couldn't span. Your
certain look fixes us both in our places
and will not fix anything. How I narrow
in your eyes to barren one, to mothered.

III. Fear of the Twenty-First Century

Transformations No. 5, Jack Shadbolt, 1976. Acrylic, latex commercial paint, black
ink, pastel, and charcoal on illustration board.

Yes, she is here, she is real –

    she smells of iron afterbirth; her mad

        red wingflaps knock loose chunks of dirt,

            shit, the hundred shades of myth.

        She's the mess you were punished

      in school for making, she

    thinks herself resplendent, she thinks herself

important. What have you given into the air?

You've gone too far and already

    she's beyond you. No one will rest.

        Not content to let you be the chrysalis

            that's left, she breaks you as herself

in fragments, she does not recognize

any of our shut-tight shapes. Nightmare

the caterpillar had, mouth made of wings,

salamander come through fire,

she bursts into bits of flag and firecracker.

Father basks in her quick-given

flame and says he has created.

If she came to me I could not

give my meagre breast to suck, I would want

her every colour for myself and she would laugh

with her worm-mouth she will devour

the world as she must.

The first line of "*Come to the edge of the barn the property really begins there*" is from "37 Haiku" in *A Wave* by John Ashbery. Copyright © 1984 by John Ashbery. All rights reserved.

The title *Seawolf Inside Its Own Dorsal Fin* is used with permission of the artist, Robert Davidson.

The opening quotation for "Red Stiletto" is from "Our Angelic Ancestor" in *Dime-Store Alchemy: The Art of Joseph Cornell* by Charles Simic. Copyright © 1992 by Charles Simic. Reprinted by permission of The Ecco Press.

In "Assonance," the line "*Hurt bird in dirt*" was adapted from an unpublished poem by Christopher Patton.

The italicized text in "Edge of the River" was adapted from informational signs in the Arboretum in Odell Park, Fredericton.

The photograph that inspired "Virginia Woolf's Mother in the Blurred Garden" depicts Julia Margaret Cameron's niece, Mrs. Herbert Duckworth. Later known as Mrs. Leslie Stephen, she was the mother of Virginia Woolf.

The National Gallery of Canada's Library and Archives, particularly the clipping files, were indispensable in my research for "*Deux personnages dans la nuit*," as were Madeleine (Beaulieu) Samson's personal reflections on Lemieux as a teacher. Books by Guy Robert (*Lemieux*, Stanké, 1975), Marie Carani (*Jean Paul Lemieux*, Musée du Québec, 1992), and Marcel Dubé (*Jean Paul Lemieux et le livre*, Art Global, 1993) aided my research.

ACKNOWLEDGEMENTS

Poems in this book have previously appeared or will soon appear, often in different forms, in the following journals and anthologies: *Arc, The Backwater Review, Breathing Fire: Canada's New Poets* (Harbour Publishing), *Bywords, Canadian Literature, Contemporary Verse 2, Dandelion, Ellipse, Event, The Fiddlehead, The Malahat Review, Meltwater: Fiction and Poetry from the Banff Centre for the Arts* (Banff Centre Press), *NeWest Review, PRISM international, A Room at the Heart of Things* (Véhicule Press), *Versodove* (Italy) and *We All Begin in a Little Magazine: Arc and the Promise of Canada's Poets, 1978 to 1998* (Arc magazine and Carleton University Press). An excerpt from "Many Have Written Poems About Blackberries" was part of the B.C. Poetry in Transit project. Some poems from "Inside a Tent of Skin" appeared in *Inside a Tent of Skin: 9 Poems from the National Gallery of Canada*, a limited-edition chapbook published by {m}Öthêr Tøñgué Press in May 1998.

"Deux personnages dans la nuit" was one of two winners of *The Malahat Review*'s long poem competition in 1997, and a selection of poems from "Inside a Tent of Skin" won first prize in {m}Öthêr Tøñgué Press's chapbook competition in 1998. "Poems for the Flood" won first prize in *Contemporary Verse 2*'s 1996/97 poetry contest. Some of the poems in this book were part of the winning manuscript in the 1996 Bronwen Wallace Award competition.

Thanks to the Canada Council for the Arts, the Ontario Arts Council, and the Regional Municipality of Ottawa-Carleton, all of which provided invaluable assistance in the writing of this book. Thanks to the Banff Centre for the Arts for time and space.

I am grateful to the many people who have read these poems and supported their development. Special thanks, for inspired and incisive critiques, to Barbara Nickel, Christopher Patton, Michael Harris, Diana Brebner, Don Coles, George McWhirter, Rhea Tregebov, and Don McKay, my editor. Thanks also to all my friends who make the writing life so worthwhile, especially Sara Graefe, Shirley Mahood, Caroline Davis Goodwin, Carmine Starnino, Tim Bowling, Keith Maillard, Craig Burnett, Peter Eastwood, Shannon Stewart, and Eleonore Schönmaier.

Thank you, as always, to my family.